100+ Dirty Jokes!

LOL FUNNY JOKES CLUB

ISBN-13: 978-1514190630
ISBN-10: 151419063X

DEDICATION

This book is dedicated to all those folks out there that love a good laugh. Dirty jokes have their place in a squeaky clean world!

CONTENTS

ACKNOWLEDGMENTS

Yeah some of these jokes are pretty dirty. If you are easily offended then you probably shouldn't read this book. For those that enjoy dirty jokes… You will love this book!

DIRTY JOKES

Q: What do a hurricane, a tornado, and a redneck divorce all have in common?

A: Someone is going to lose their trailer.

Q: Why is divorce so expensive?

A: Because it's worth it.

Q: What is the difference between medium and rare?

A: Six inches is medium, eight inches is rare.

Q: What do a clitoris, an anniversary, and a toilet have in common?

A: Men usually miss all three.

Q: How are men are like cement?

A: After getting laid, they take a long time to get hard.

Q: What do a coffin and a condom have in common?

A: They're both filled with stiffs. One is coming and one is going.

Q: What are the small bumps around a woman's nipples for?

A: It's braille for suck here.

Q: Why don't men fake orgasm?

A: Because no man would pull those faces on purpose.

Q: Why do women rub their eyes when they get up in the morning?

A: They don't have balls to scratch.

Q: Why do women have tits?
A: So men will talk to them.

Q: What does a 75-year-old woman have between her breasts that a 25-year-old doesn't?
A: Her belly button.

Q: How are women and rocks alike?
A: You skip across the flat ones.

Q: Why do men find it difficult to make eye contact?
A: Because breasts don't have eyes.

Q: How do you tell when a blonde reaches orgasm?
A: She drops her nail-file!

Q: What's the difference between a blonde and a brick?
A: When you lay a brick it doesn't follow you around for two weeks whining.

Q: What is the best blonde secretary in the world to have?

A: One that never misses a period.

Q: What's the difference between a counterfeit dollar and a skinny blonde?

A: One is a phony buck.

Q: What do blondes do after they comb their hair?

A: They pull up their pants.

Q: What's the difference between a chorus line of blondes and a magician?

A: A magician has a cunning array of stunts.

Q: How does the blonde turn on the light after she has had sex?

A: She opens the car door.

Q: What do you call a blonde lesbian?

A: A waste.

Q: Why did God give blondes 2% more brains than horses?
A: Because he didn't want them shitting in the streets during parades.

Q: How does a blonde moonwalk?
A: She pulls down her panties and slides her ass along the floor!

Q: How do you know a blonde has just lost her virginity?
A: Her crayons are still sticky.

Q: What does a blonde and a turtle have in common?
A: If either one of them end up on their back they are both f*cked!

Q: What is 61 to a blonde?
A: She wants 8 (ate) more.

Q: How come blondes can't water ski?
A: When they get their crotch wet they think they have to lie down.

Q: How do you get a blonde pregnant?

A: Come in her shoes and let the flies do the rest.

Q: What's the difference between a 90 year old woman and a computer?

A: A 90 year old woman won't accept a three-and-a-half-inch floppy.

Q: Did you hear about the new blonde paint?

A: It's not real bright. But it's cheap and it spreads easy.

Q: What do a dildo and soy beans have in common?

A: They are both substitute meats.

Q: How are blondes like pianos?

A: When they aren't upright, they are grand.

Q: Why do blondes like tilt steering?

A: More head room.

Q: How do you get a blonde off of your knees?

A: Come.

Q: How do you know a blonde likes you?

A: She screws you two nights in a row.

Q: Why don't blondes like anal sex?

A: They don't like their brains being screwed with.

Q: What did one saggy boob say to the other saggy boob?

A: If we don't get some support soon, people are going to think we are nuts.

Q: Are birth control pills deductible?

A: Only if they don't work.

Q: How do you know you're leading a sad life?

A: When a nymphomaniac tells you, "Let's just be friends."

Q: How many men does it take to put the toilet seat down?

A: Nobody knows because it hasn't happened yet.

Q: What's the new Italian airline that flies out of Geno?

A: It's called Genitali.

Q: Why do men masturbate?

A: It is sex with someone they love.

Q: What did the hurricane say to the coconut tree?

A: Hold onto your nuts. This is no ordinary blow job!

Q: What did Adam say to Eve?

A: Stand back, I don't know how big this thing gets!

Q: What do you get when you cross an owl and a rooster?

A: A cock that stays up all night.

Q: Why don't bunnies make noise when they make love?

A: Because they have cotton balls.

Q: Why were men given larger brains than dogs?

A: So they wouldn't hump women's legs at cocktail parties.

Q: What are the two greatest lies?

A: The check is in the mail, and I promise I won't cum in your mouth.

Q: What's long, hard, and has semen in it?

A: A submarine!

Q: What's organic dental floss?

A: Pubic hair!

Q: What did the banana say to the vibrator?

A: I don't know why you're shaking, she's going to eat me!

Q: What's the difference between a penis and a bonus?

A: Your wife will always blow your bonus!

Q: Why did the condom cross the road?

A: Because it was pissed off.

Q: What is the difference between a drug pusher and a prostitute?

A: A prostitute can wash her crack and sell it again.

Q: How did Dairy Queen get pregnant?

A: Burger King didn't cover his whopper.

Q: What happens if you put the Energizer Bunny's batteries in backwards?

A: He keeps coming and coming and coming!

Q: What did the egg say to the boiling water?

A: It might take me a while to get hard. I just got laid last night.

Q: Why don't women blink during foreplay?

A: They don't have time.

Q: Why is it called a Wonder Bra?

A: When she takes it off, you wonder where her tits went.

Q: What is the difference between a frog and a horny toad?

A: One says ribbit ribbit, the other one says rub-it, rub-it!

Q: What's the difference between a rooster and a hooker?

A: a rooster says cocka-doodle-doo and a hooker says any cock will do.

Q: Why did Frosty the Snowman pull down his pants?

A: He heard the snow blower coming.

Q: What did the egg say to the boiling water?

A: How can you expect me to get hard so fast? I just got laid a minute ago.

Q: Why is air a lot like sex?

A: Because it's no big deal unless you're not getting any.

Q: How many divorcees does it take to change a light bulb?

A: None. The sockets all went with the house.

Q: Did you hear about the lawyer whose divorce ended up in a nasty custody fight about a dog?

A: When the lawyer won, the dog bit him.

Q: What do a pizza delivery man and a gynecologist have in common?

A: Both can smell it but can't eat it.

Q: What did Bill Clinton say to Monica?

A: I told you to lick my erection, not wreck my election.

Q: What do a hurricane, a tornado, a fire and a divorce have in common?

A: They are four ways you can lose your house!

Q: What do you get when you mix a rooster with a telephone pole?

A: A 30 foot cock that wants to reach out and touch someone.

Q: Why is being in the military like a blow job?

A: The closer you get to discharge, the better you feel.

Q: What does a woman's asshole do when she is having an orgasm?

A: He is usually home with the kids!

Q: Why are men like laxatives?

A: They irritate the shit out of you.

Q: What's the difference between a blonde and a phone booth?

A: You need a quarter to use the phone.

Q: What's the difference between a blonde and a broom closet?

A: Only two men fit inside a broom closet at once.

Q: What is that insensitive bit at the base of the penis called?

A: The man.

Q: What did the blonde do when she got her period?

A: Looked around for the bastard that must have shot her.

Q: What does the Bermuda Triangle and blondes have in common?
A: They've both swallowed a lot of semen.

Q: What do you call a blonde with ESP and PMS?
A: A know-it-all bitch.

Q: How is a penis like fishing?
A: The small ones you throw back, the medium ones you eat, and the larger ones you mount.

Q: Why do men have a hole in their penis?
A: So they can think with an open mind.

Q: Moms have Mother's Day and fathers have Father's Day. What do single guys have?
A: Palm Sunday.

Q: How is a man like a snowstorm?

A: You never know when he's coming, how many inches you'll get, or how long it will last.

Q: What do men and sperm have in common?

A: They both have a one-in-a-million chance of becoming a human being.

Q: Why is a man's pee yellow and his sperm white?

A: So he can tell if he is coming or going.

Q: Why don't women have men's brains?

A: Because they don't have penises to put them in.

Q: What's the major cause of divorce?

A: Once is not enough.

Q: What are three two letter words that say small?

A: Is it in?

Q: What is the one thing you will never hear a man say?

A: Her tits are just too big.

Q: Did you hear about the old guy that died from a Viagra overdose?

A: They weren't able to close his casket!

Q: Have you heard about the new flavored birth control candy?

A: It is called predickamints.

Q: What do you call the best fish hook baiter?

A: A master baiter!

Q: What if... What if something bad happens?

A: What if my aunt had balls? She'd be my uncle.

Q: What did the dick say to the condom?

A: Cover me. I'm about to go in.

Q: Why did the penis go to the convenient store?

A: He wanted to get a slurpee.

Q: What does butter and a blonde have in common?

A: They've both been known to spread for bread.

Q: What comes after 69?

A: Brushing your teeth.

Q: What is 72?

A: 69 with 4 people watching.

Q: What's the difference between erotic and kinky?

A: Erotic is when you use a feather. Kinky is when you use the whole chicken.

Q: What are three words you dread the most while making love?
A: Honey, I'm home!

Q: What is it when a woman talks dirty to a man?
A: $2.99 a minute.

Q: What is it when a man talks dirty to a woman?
A: Sexual harassment.

Q: How do you find a blind man in a nudist colony?
A: It's not hard.

Q: Why are condoms like cameras?
A: They both capture the moment.

Q: What did the sign on the whore house say?
A: Beat it we are closed!

Q: You know the worst thing about oral sex?

A: The view.

Q: Why do men become smarter during sex?

A: Because they are plugged into a genius.

Q: What's one thing everybody sees in a blonde?

A: A dick.

Q: What does a screen door and a blonde have in common?

A: The more you bang it the looser it gets.

Q: Why do blondes get confused in the ladies room?

A: They have to pull their own pants down.

Q: What did the blonde say during a porno?

A: There I am!

Q: What do you call a blonde that can suck a golfball through a water hose?

A: Sweetheart!

Q: Why did the blonde guy put ice in his condom?

A: To keep the swelling down.

ABOUT THE AUTHOR

The LOL Funny Jokes Club is dedicated to comedy. We'll tickle your funny bone with our side-splitting jokes and humor. Whether it's funny one-liners hilarious jokes, or laugh-out-loud rib tickling knee slappers, the LOL Funny Jokes Club does it all!

To find more funny and hilarious joke books just search for LOL FUNNY JOKES CLUB on Amazon.com.

Made in the USA
Las Vegas, NV
05 November 2023

80295487R00021